I0504695

AI FEMALE ARCHER COLORING BOOK

Hey there, I'm Jeremy Hubert Burt. I was feeling inspired and decided to use a prompt to create some 3D coloring book pages. The prompt I used was:

"Design an awe-inspiring coloring book page featuring a fearless female archer in a fantasy world. Against a pristine white background, use bold black lines to illustrate the archer, highlighting her strength and bravery.

Create intricate and ornate background designs that reflect the archer's noble heritage and heroic accomplishments. These designs should evoke a sense of wonder and admiration.

Incorporate various shapes like delicate swirls, intricate patterns, and symbolic motifs throughout the page, enveloping the archer in a world of power and elegance. Add inspiring phrases in a font that ignites courage and determination.

Outline the archer's attire and weapons with bold black lines, clearly defining the boundaries for coloring. This allows enthusiasts to unleash their creativity and bring the archer to life using the striking contrast of black and white.

The coloring book page offers an exhilarating journey into a realm of fantasy and adventure. It invites individuals to immerse themselves in the captivating art of coloring, providing a delightful sense of relaxation and stress relief. Embody the spirit of the fearless archer against the timeless contrast of black and white."

After creating the design, I decided to edit the levels in GIMP in greyscale image mode to give it that extra touch of depth and detail. The whole process only took me a day, and I'm really happy with the results. I even published the pages using the Sqribble ebook maker, which was super easy to use. Check out the link if you want to Publish Your eBook: https://bit.ly/3nVzjvK.

jeremyburt@ishopdailyonline.com jburt_01@hotmail.com
Make Money Online: https://ishopdailyonline.com
Print On Demand: https://ishopdaily.redbubble.com
Print On Demand @ Etsy: https://ishopdailyonline.etsy.com
dj12mind Instrumental Music Albums: https://dj12mind.com
Affiliate Products: https://index.ishopdailyonline.com
Patreon: https://www.patreon.com/user?u=80194438
Facebook: https://www.facebook.com/jeremy.burt2
Youtube:
https://www.youtube.com/channel/UCwV3nApPDh3dNHUGIX4w5nA
tiktok: https://www.tiktok.com/@jeremyburt4?lang=en
amazon: https://www.amazon.com/author/jeremyburt
THANK YOU FOR CHECKING IT OUT!